ASHTON FALLS

COZY COOKBOOK

BY

KATHI DALEY

This book is a compilation of recipes created by the author or given to her by family or friends. Any resemblance to other recipes is entirely coincidental.

Copyright © 2014 by Katherine Daley

Version 1.0

All rights reserved, including the right of reproduction in whole or in part in any form.

Christmas Eve in Ashton Falls

Christmas in Ashton Falls is a special time of year when the entire community comes together to decorate and enjoy everything the town has to offer. The snow is falling gently on the busy sidewalk as holiday shoppers scurry from one brightly lit store to the next. I know this may seem odd, but while I like to complete the bulk of my shopping early, every Christmas Eve I make a solitary trip into town to shop for people I have never met and will most likely never meet.

The tradition began when I was just a small child. My grandmother and I attended morning services on Christmas Eve at the Ashton Falls Community Church. After the service ended the pastor mentioned to my grandmother that he'd just been informed about a family in need. My grandmother, who was the type to help anyone anytime, immediately volunteered to provide what she could for the family. I had plans of my own with my best friends, Levi and Ellie, but Grandma insisted that Christmas was about giving to those who crossed our paths. I wasn't happy about it but I canceled my plans and the two of us went into town.

Neither Grandma nor I had ever met this family, but we had a handwritten note letting us know what type of gifts they'd requested. Most of the items were practical, such as a warm winter coat and heavy wool socks. I hadn't wanted to be bothered with the errand, but as we shopped for people we would never meet, I found a deep joy that I didn't even know I was missing. That special shopping trip turned into an annual event for the two of us, and now that I'm an adult, I continue the tradition in memory of the special woman who taught a little girl the true meaning of Christmas.

APPETIZERS

Pizza Rolls

Bacon Herb Cheeseball

Chicken and Green Chili Dip

Artichoke Dip

Chipped Beef Dip

Beefy Nachos

Crab and Artichoke Dip

Buffalo Chicken Appetizer Pizza

Pizza Rolls

1 loaf frozen bread thawed
½ cup grated mozzarella cheese
½ cup grated cheddar cheese

4 oz. pepperoni (or other pizza topping)
3 tbs. butter, melted
½ cup grated Parmesan cheese

Roll a loaf of the bread so that it's flat. Place mozzarella cheese, cheddar cheese, and pepperoni in center. Fold in both ends of loaf and then roll so that seam is on the bottom.

Slice rolls into 12 pieces and place in greased 9 x 13 baking pan. Brush butter over the top of each roll. Sprinkle with Parmesan cheese.

Let rise until double in size.

Bake at 375 degrees for 15–20 minutes.

Serve with ranch or bleu cheese dressing for dipping.

Bacon Herb Cheeseball

12 oz. cream cheese, softened
6 pieces bacon, cooked crisp and crumbled
1 can (4 oz.) diced green chilis
1 tbs. chopped garlic
1 tbs. chopped fresh basil
1 tbs. chopped chives
1 cup grated Parmesan cheese
1 cup grated Jack cheese
1 cup grated cheddar cheese
2 tsp. horseradish
⅔ cup chopped almonds

Mix all ingredients except almonds in a bowl. I just use my hands to mix everything together. Form a ball. Lay almonds on a breadboard. Roll cheeseball in almonds until coated.

Wrap in plastic wrap and chill overnight. Serve with crackers.

Chicken and Green Chili Dip

Combine in large bowl:

2 large chicken breasts, cooked and cubed
2 cups artichoke hearts, chopped
8 oz. cream cheese, softened
I cup grated Parmesan cheese
1 cup Pepper Jack cheese, grated
1 cup cheddar cheese, grated
14 oz. diced green chiles (Ortega)
1 cup mayonnaise
Salt and pepper to taste

Pour into 9 x 13 pan. Top with additional grated cheese (as much as you want).

Bake at 350 degrees until bubbly, about 45 minutes.

Serve with chips, crackers, French bread slices, or tortillas.

Artichoke Dip

2 cans (approx. 15 oz. each) artichoke hearts, drained and diced
1 can (approx. 7 oz.) Ortega or other diced green chili
1 cup mayonnaise
2½ cups grated Parmesan cheese

Mix everything in a square baking dish and bake at 425 degrees for 35–40 minutes until bubbly and slightly brown on top.
Serve hot with French bread or tortilla chips.

Chipped Beef Dip

16 oz. sour cream
8 oz. cream cheese, softened
1 can jalapeños (or more if you like it really hot)
1 large jar of dried beef, rinsed and chopped

Mix ingredients above. Bake at 350 degrees for 1 hour

Serve with French bread squares or tortilla chips.

Beefy Nachos

Make meat the day before your football gathering.
Trim all fat off boneless rib roast (size depends on amount of meat desired). Season with salt, pepper, and garlic powder. Place in slow cooker. Cover meat with store-bought salsa, either hot or mild, depending on preference.

Cook on high until meat begins to pull apart. Continue to shred meat as it cooks. When it's completely done (cooking time depends on size of meat and heat of slow cooker, but about 8 hours), spoon meat from sauce with slotted spoon. Refrigerate.

Next day:

Layer tortilla chips on cookie sheet. Cover with grated cheese; I use sharp cheddar and Jack, but you can use whatever.

Place cookie sheet under broiler with heat set on low.

Reheat the meat on stove or in microwave; when cheese is melted on tortilla chips cover with meat — be sure it's drained of excess fluid — serve with sour cream, guacamole, diced tomatoes, or whatever you'd like to add.

Crab and Artichoke Dip

8 oz. cream cheese, softened

8 oz. Havarti cheese, grated

2 cans (approx. 14 oz. each) artichoke hearts, diced

8 oz. crab meat, fresh or canned

2 cups Parmesan cheese, grated

1 cup sour cream

2 tsp. horseradish (add more if you like it hot)

Mix and bake at 450 degrees for 30–45 minutes; stir after 20 minutes.

Serve with baguette slices, tortilla chips, or crackers.

Buffalo Chicken Appetizer Pizza

4 tortillas
1 jar Alfredo sauce, any brand
4 cups mozzarella cheese, shredded
2 chicken breasts, cooked, cubed, and tossed with Frank's RedHot Buffalo Wing Sauce
1 can artichoke hearts, diced (approx. 14 oz.)
1 can spinach (approx. 14 oz.)
1 cup grated Parmesan cheese

Makes 4 servings

For each serving:

1 large flour tortilla, toasted (I put it on a sandwich grill, but you can toast in oven)

Cover with:

2 tbs. Alfredo sauce (you can use more or less per your taste)
1 cup mozzarella cheese
½ prepared chicken breast
¼ can artichoke hearts
¼ can spinach, squeezed of excess liquid
Sprinkle with grated Parmesan to taste

Bake in 350-degree oven for 15 minutes or until cheese is melted and toppings are heated.

Note: you can leave off the chicken for a vegetarian variety or replace toppings with pepperoni, olives, mushrooms, whatever your taste. You can also replace the Alfredo sauce with pizza sauce.

One of my favorite things to do on Christmas Eve is to view the windows along Main Street. If you view the windows in order from west to east they tell a story that's slightly different every year. This year the story is about a young boy who hopes to find the perfect Christmas gift for his mother, who has been forced to stay at home as she awaits the birth of his new baby sister. His mom has endured a difficult pregnancy and her spirits are at an all-time low, but the little boy knows deep in his heart that if he can just find the right gift, everything will turn out okay. Although the child has but a few pennies he managed to earn doing odd jobs, he's determined to find the one gift that will make his mom smile. Each of the windows tells the story of the boy as he embarks on his journey. Many of the displays feature the shops the boy visited in search of his gift, but other demonstrate the side tours he takes along the way. My favorite window this year re-creates the park where he followed a stray dog who had been living under a bridge. The dog and the boy spend some time playing before the boy realizes he should be on his way. The story ends with the boy standing in front of the nativity scene at the local church. As he contemplates the meaning of the scene, he realizes that the best gift you can give comes not from a store but from the heart.

Muffins and Sweet Breads

Pumpkin Patch Muffins

Zak's Easy Sticky Buns

Banana Macadamia Nut Muffins

Apple Pie Biscuits

Amaretto Pumpkin Bread

Cranberry Muffins

Pumpkin Patch Muffins

3 cups sugar
1 cup vegetable oil
4 eggs
1 16 oz. can pumpkin (2 cups)
½ cup water
3½ cups flour
2 tsp. baking soda
1 tsp. baking powder
½ tsp. salt
1 tbs. cinnamon
1 tsp. ginger
1 tsp. ground nutmeg
½ tsp. ground cloves
½ tsp. all spice
4 cups walnuts chopped

Combine sugar, oil, and eggs. Add pumpkin and water and mix well.

Combine dry ingredients and add to pumpkin mixture. Add nuts.

Spoon into greased cupcake pans (or use papers).
Bake at 350 degrees for 28–30 minutes.

Cream Cheese Frosting (optional):
¾ cup of butter, softened
6 oz. cream cheese, softened
1 tsp. vanilla
3 cups powdered sugar

Whip all ingredients together and spread on to cooled muffins.

Zak's Easy Sticky Buns

Take 6 tbs. butter and melt in a pan. When melted add ¾ cup brown sugar and ¼ cup corn syrup. Stir mixture over medium low heat, bringing to a boil.

When at a full boil remove from heat. Do not over- boil. The syrup will set up to hard.

Pour into the bottom of a 9 x 13-inch pan. Add ¾ cup of chopped pecans on top of the syrup mixture. Set aside.

In a pie pan, melt 4 tbs. butter. In a separate pie pan, mix ½ cup sugar and 1½ tbs. cinnamon. Set aside.

Take 1½ loaves of thawed frozen bread dough and cut into 12 equal pieces. Take each piece and roll into a tube. Take each piece of dough and roll first into the melted butter and then in the cinnamon sugar. Tie the piece into a knot and set in the prepared baking pan on top of the syrup pecan mixture.

Put the rolls in a warm place to rise until they fill the pan.

Bake at 400 degrees for 20–25 minutes. The rolls are done when they're nice and brown. Make sure the rolls are cooked through. Do not undercook.

When the rolls are baked, take out the pan. Cover the top of the pan with a foil-lined cookie sheet. Invert the pan onto the cookie sheet. The pecan mixture will seep down on top of the rolls.

Serve warm.

Makes 1 dozen.

Banana Macadamia Nut Muffins

1¼ cups mashed ripe bananas (about 3 large)
½ cup sugar
¼ cup dark brown sugar, firmly packed
½ cup (1 stick) butter, melted
¼ cup milk
1 large egg
1½ cups flour
1½ tsp. baking soda
¼ tsp. salt
½ tsp. ground nutmeg
½ tsp. cinnamon
2 cups macadamia nuts, toasted, chopped

Preheat oven to 350 degrees. Grease 12 muffin cups or line with muffin papers. Combine bananas, both sugars, butter, milk, and egg in large bowl. Mix in flour, baking soda, and spices. Fold in half of nuts. Divide batter among prepared muffin cups. Sprinkle tops of muffins with remaining macadamia nuts. Bake until muffins are golden brown and tester inserted into center comes out clean, about 25 minutes.

Apple Pie Biscuits

Preheat oven to 375 degrees.
Spray a 6 x 9 baking dish on all sides with nonstick spray.
Open 1 can large buttermilk biscuits (I use Pillsbury Grands!).
Melt 1 stick (½ cup) butter (I melt it in a bowl in the microwave).

Combine in a bowl:
½ cup white sugar
½ cup brown sugar
1 tsp. nutmeg
1 tbs. cinnamon

Prepare biscuits:
Dip each biscuit into butter coating on both sides, then dip each biscuit into sugar mixture, coating on both sides. Place into baking dish.

The topping:
Top with one can of apple pie filling.

Combine remaining butter with remaining sugar mixture. Add ½ cup oatmeal and 1 cup chopped pecans. Pour over top of biscuits.

Bake at 375 degrees for 35 minutes.

Drizzle over top when baked:
Combine:
1 cup powdered sugar
¼ cup heavy cream
Serve hot.

Amaretto Pumpkin Bread

1 cup flour
¼ cup brown sugar, packed
1 tsp. baking powder
1 tsp. ground cinnamon
½ tsp. ginger
¼ tsp. baking soda
¼ cup molasses
¼ cup pumpkin
1 egg
3 tsp. butter, softened
2 tbs. milk
½ cup chopped walnuts

Combine above ingredients until well blended. Pour into greased bread pan and bake at 350 degrees for 25 minutes. Remove from pan and let cool.

Frosting:

½ cup powdered sugar
1 tbs. amaretto

Mix well, then drizzle over top. Garnish with additional chopped walnuts.

Cranberry Muffins

Combine in large bowl:

2 cups flour
1 cup sugar
1½ tsp. baking powder
1 tsp. ground nutmeg
1 tsp. ground cinnamon
½ tsp. ground ginger
½ tsp. baking soda
½ tsp. salt

Cut in:

1 stick butter

Add:

¾ cup orange juice
2 eggs, beaten
1 tbs. vanilla extract

Fold in:

1½ cups cranberries, chopped
2 cups pecans, chopped

Bake in greased muffin cups at 375 degrees for about 20 minutes (toothpick should come out clean). Cool.

I bought my gifts and viewed the windows before heading over to Zoe's Zoo, the wild and domestic animal rescue and rehabilitation shelter I run. I've always wanted to come down to the Zoo at midnight on Christmas Eve to see if the animals do in fact talk to one another. My guess is that they do, and how wonderful it would be to hear what they had to say. I imagine the bear cubs who are staying with us for the winter would tell me to keep it down because they're trying to sleep, and the kittens in residence would talk about what fun it would be to climb the Christmas tree my assistants, Jeremy and Tiffany, had erected in the lobby. The dogs who are visiting would most likely want to have a chat to ensure that I'd find them forever homes with wonderful people who would love them as much as they had always loved the humans in their lives.

Soups, Stews, Chili, and Chowder

Timberland Shrimp Chowder

Cheesy Chicken Chowder

Mountain Man Beef Stew

Grandma Donovan's Cheesy Potato Soup

Easy Vegetarian Black Bean Chili

Rosie's Clam Chowder

White Bean Chili

Cheesy Ham and Potato Soup

Next-Day Turkey Soup

Timberland Shrimp Chowder

Base:

1 stick butter
½ chopped onion (or more if you like onion)
3-4 cloves garlic chopped
6 cups peeled and diced potato (frozen hash browns work as well)
2 lbs. cooked shrimp (any size; Rosie uses medium, but she has used salad shrimp in a pinch)
32 oz. chicken broth (can use part chicken broth and part water if preferred)

Spices: amounts can be adjusted to accommodate taste.

¼ tsp. chili powder
¼ tsp. cayenne pepper
¼ tsp. ground cumin
¼ tsp. coriander
½ tsp. nutmeg
½ tsp. paprika
1 tsp. salt
1 tsp. white pepper

Melt butter in heavy pan. Sauté onion and garlic.
Add potatoes and shrimp.
Cover with chicken broth (just enough to boil potatoes). Add spices.
Boil until potatoes are tender; this time will vary depending on the size of potato cubes.

Cheese sauce:
While potatoes are boiling, use a separate pan to make cheese sauce.

1 stick butter
4 oz. cream cheese (1 small or ½ large pkg.)
1 cup heavy cream
2 cups shredded cheddar cheese (do not use non or low fat)
2 cups grated Parmesan cheese (or 1 cup Parmesan and 1 cup Romano)

Melt butter in pan over medium heat. Add cream cheese. Stir until melted. Add cream. Add cheese a little at a time.

After potatoes are tender, slowly fold cheese sauce into base. Stir constantly until well blended.

Cheesy Chicken Chowder

3 cups chicken broth
2 cups diced potatoes
1 cup diced carrots
1 cup diced celery
½ cup diced onion
Salt
Pepper
¼ cup butter
⅓ cup flour
2 cups heavy cream
2 cups shredded cheddar
2 cups cooked and cubed chicken

Bring chicken broth to a boil. Reduce heat. Add potatoes, carrots, celery, salt, and pepper. Cover and simmer until vegetables are tender.

Meanwhile, melt butter in saucepan. Add flour and mix well. Gradually stir in cream. Cook over low heat until slightly thickened. Stir in cheese. Heat until melted. Add broth along with chicken. Cook over low heat until warmed through.

Mountain Man Beef Stew

2 lbs. boneless chuck cut into cubes (or precut stew meat)
Seasoned salt, garlic powder, and pepper
2 tbs. vegetable oil
3 large baking potatoes cut into cubes
1 large onion, peeled and chopped
4 large carrots cut into bite-size pieces

3 tbs. flour
1 cup beef broth
1 cup burgundy wine (or other red)
3 bay leaves
1 tsp. basil
1 cup sliced mushrooms
1 can artichoke hearts, quartered

Season meat with salt, garlic powder, and pepper, then brown beef in hot vegetable oil. Add all the vegetables except mushrooms and artichoke hearts. Sauté over medium heat for about 5 minutes. Sprinkle flour over meat and vegetables and stir to coat. Add broth, wine, bay leaves, and basil. Bring to a boil and then cover and lower heat. Simmer for about 1½ hours until vegetables are tender. Add mushrooms and artichokes during last half hour.

Grandma Donovan's Cheesy Potato Soup

12 cups potatoes, peeled and diced
1 bunch leeks or green onions, washed and chopped
8 cups chicken broth
4 chicken bouillon cubes

Boil until potatoes are tender. Mash potatoes into small chunks in broth. Do not drain.

Lower heat and add:

1 stick butter
1 8 oz. pkg. cream cheese
2 cups heavy whipping cream

When cream cheese is completely dissolved add:

8 cups shredded cheddar cheese
2 cups grated Parmesan cheese
Salt and pepper to taste

Simmer until cheese is melted and soup thickens.

Notes:

Add cheese slowly, stirring constantly until blended.
You can add broccoli, cauliflower, or both for variety.
This soup makes a *lot* but is good as a leftover. In fact, many times Grandma made the soup the day before, refrigerated it, and then reheated.

Easy Vegetarian Black Bean Chili

Sauté in small amount of olive oil:

1 bell pepper, diced
1 onion, diced
2 cloves garlic, chopped

Add:

1 tsp. cumin
1 tsp. oregano
2 tsp. chili powder

Add:

1 tub salsa (I use hot, but you can use mild)
1 15-oz. can black beans, drained

Cook on medium heat until warm.

Serve with rice and tortillas.

Rosie's Clam Chowder

1 lb. bacon
1 cup chopped leeks
1 cup chopped yellow onion
1 carrot, peeled and diced
Salt and pepper
1 tbs. chopped fresh thyme
½ cup flour
1 lb. potatoes, peeled and diced
4 cups clam juice
2 cups heavy cream
2 lbs. littleneck clams, chopped
Parsley for garnish

In heavy pot, fry bacon until crispy. Stir in leeks, onion, and carrots. Sauté for about 2 minutes. Season with salt and pepper. Add thyme. Stir in flour and cook for 2 minutes. Add the potatoes. Stir in clam juice and bring to boil. Reduce to a simmer. Simmer until potatoes are tender and then add the cream. Bring to simmer and add clams.

Garnish with parsley and serve in bread bowls.

White Bean Chili

4 chicken breasts, cubed
Sauté in olive oil until chicken is cooked through.

Add:
1 onion, diced
2 carrots, diced
2 stalks celery, diced
2 cloves garlic, diced

Sauté until veggies are tender.

Add to chicken mixture:
2 cans Great Northern White Beans
1 can chicken broth
2 cans diced Ortega Green Chiles
1 tsp. salt
1 tsp. cumin
1 tsp. oregano
1 tsp. pepper
1 tsp. cayenne pepper (or more if you like it hot)

Cook over medium heat until warm.

Stir in:
1 cup sour cream
½ cup heavy whipping cream

Heat for a few more minutes.

Serve with tortillas.

Cheesy Ham and Potato Soup

Combine in stockpot:

4 large potatoes (8–9 cups), washed, peeled, and cubed
2–3 large carrots, washed and sliced
1 small onion, finely chopped
4 cups cooked ham, cubed
8 cups chicken broth

Bring to boil and cook until potatoes are tender.

In separate pan:
Melt 1 stick of butter (½ cup).
Add 3 cups of heavy cream.
Add 3 cups of grated cheddar cheese.
Slowly add 1 cup of Parmesan cheese.
Salt and pepper to taste.

When potatoes are cooked through, break them up with a fork or masher. Slowly add cream mixture, stirring constantly.

I use additional Parmesan to thicken or additional milk to thin, if needed.

Next-Day Turkey Soup

1 leftover turkey breast carcass
3 qt. water
3 tbs. chicken bouillon granules
1 cup uncooked instant rice
2 cups sliced carrots
1 cup chopped onion
1 cup sliced celery
1 clove garlic, minced
Salt and pepper to taste
1 cup turkey meat, cubed
2 tbs. fresh parsley, minced

Place carcass, water, and bouillon granules in heavy pot and bring to a boil. Reduce heat, cover, and simmer for 1½ hours. Remove carcass.

Remove meat from bones and set aside. Discard bones, then strain broth and skim fat.

Add rice to broth and bring to a boil; reduce heat and simmer for 30 minutes.

Add carrots, onion, celery, garlic, salt, and pepper and simmer 25 minutes or longer (vegetables should be tender). Add cubed turkey, plus meat removed from carcass and parsley. Heat through.

After stopping at the Zoo to spend some time with my animal friends I returned home to my fiancé, Zak, and our own animals, Charlie, Bella, Marlow, and Spade. Charlie is my best friend and confidant. He has been with me through thick and thin and I really don't know what I'd do without him. Bella is Zak's dog, a large bundle of fur who was displaced when her mom was forced into a retirement home. Marlow and Spade are both rescues I brought home at one point. The animals and I headed upstairs to wrap the last few gifts I picked up while I was shopping that morning. Marlow loved to unroll the ribbon and Spade will crawl into any box or bag he comes across. Bella seems content to watch the festivities from her bed near the fireplace, and Charlie, like always, lends a paw to help when it comes time to tie up the ribbons. As my animal friends and I share a quiet Christmas Eve moment, I take a breath to embrace the smell of the pies Zak has baking in the kitchen. I know my family and friends will be arriving in a few moments, but for now, in the instant, I will embrace the quiet.

Mains and Sides

Cheesy White Chicken Enchiladas

Zak's Easy Mac and Cheese

Ellie's Fettuccine Alfredo

Zoe's Chicken Tortilla Casserole

Hazel's Frito Bean Dish

Italian Beef Sandwiches

Ellie's Ground Beef Stroganoff

Twice Baked Potato Casserole

Zoe's Quick and Easy Hash Brown Casserole

Scalloped Ham and Potato Casserole

Pulled Pork Verde

Loco Moco

Chicken and Rice

Cheesy White Chicken Enchiladas

Preheat oven to 350 degrees. Spray 9 x 13 baking dish with nonstick spray.

Mix in a bowl:

3 large chicken breasts, cooked and cubed
1 cup sour cream
8 oz. diced green chiles (Ortega)

Fill 8 medium flour tortillas with chicken filling.

Sauce:

In a medium saucepan combine:
1 stick butter, melted over medium heat
4 oz. cream cheese, added to melted butter and stirred until smooth
1 cup heavy whipping cream, stirred until blended
1½ cups grated parmesan, stirred in slowly to avoid lumps

Pour over tortillas and top with 16 oz. Monterey Jack cheese, grated.
Bake uncovered at 350 degrees for 20–25 minutes.
Broil for a few minutes to brown.

Zak's Easy Mac and Cheese

1 box (16 oz.) penne pasta
4 chicken breasts, cooked and cubed
1 can of Campbell's Cream of Cheddar soup
1 can of Campbell's Nacho Cheese soup
(you can use two cans of either if you like your casserole more or less spicy)

2 cups shredded cheddar cheese
1 cup grated Parmesan cheese
1 jar (16 oz.) Alfredo sauce (any brand)
¾ cup milk
1 cup cashews (or more if you'd like)
Salt and pepper to taste
Cheddar cheese crackers

Boil pasta according to directions on box (10–12 minutes).

Meanwhile, mix cooked and cubed chicken, soups, cheeses, Alfredo sauce, milk, cashews, and salt and pepper together in a large bowl.

Drain pasta when tender and add to chicken mixture. Stir until well mixed.

Pour into a greased 9 x 13 baking pan. Top with crumbled cheddar cheese crackers.

Bake at 350 degrees for 30 minutes.

Ellie's Fettuccine Alfredo

Melt 1 stick butter (real butter, no substitutions) in saucepan over medium heat.

When melted add:
½ 8 oz. pkg. cream cheese
2 cups heavy whipping cream
Stir until cream cheese is completely dissolved.

Slowly add:
1½ cups grated Parmesan cheese (the good stuff)
1 cup grated Romano cheese (add slowly; don't let it clump)
Stir until smooth.

Add:
1 tsp. ground nutmeg
½ tsp. garlic powder
Add salt and pepper to taste (Ellie uses white pepper).

Note: if you like your sauce thicker you can add additional Parmesan, and if you like it thinner you can add additional cream.
Pour over fettuccine, tortellini, or any other pasta (fresh from the refrigerator section is best).

Zoe's Chicken Tortilla Casserole

4 chicken breasts, cooked and cubed
2 cans (7 oz.) diced green chilis (Zoe uses Ortega)
1 can (10 oz.) chicken broth
1 can (10 oz.) cream of mushroom soup
1 can (10 oz.) cream of chicken soup
1 large can or 2 small cans sliced black olives
1 can (15 oz.) corn drained

Combine everything above and set aside.

1 pkg. corn tortillas
2 cups shredded cheddar cheese

Layer half of tortillas, half of soup, and half of cheese in greased 9 x 13 baking pan.

Repeat with second half.

Bake at 350 degrees for 30 minutes.

Hazel's Frito Bean Dish

1 can (15 oz.) chili with beans (any brand)
½ chopped onion
1 can (7 oz.) chopped green chilis (Hazel uses Ortega)
1 can (4 oz.) sliced black olives
1 can (10 oz.) Campbell's Nacho Cheese soup

Mix everything above together.

1 bag FRITOS (plain or Chili Cheese).

Layer chili mixture with FRITOS in greased baking pan.

Bake at 350 degrees for 30 minutes.

Italian Beef Sandwiches

1 boneless chuck roast (3–4 lbs.), trimmed of fat and cut in half
3 tbs. dried basil
3 tbs. dried oregano
1 cup water
1 envelope onion soup mix
I cup mozzarella grated
Italian rolls (or other rolls)

Place roast in slow cooker. Add water and spices. Pour soup over top. Cover and cook 7–8 hours.

Shred meat spoon onto Italian rolls. Sprinkle mozzarella over the top. Broil until cheese is golden.

Ellie's Ground Beef Stroganoff

Brown 1 lb. of ground beef.

Add 4 cloves of garlic, chopped.
Add ½ onion, chopped.
Salt and pepper to taste.

When meat is brown, add:

16 oz. sour cream
5 cups sliced mushrooms
4 oz. cream cheese
½ cup soy sauce
½ cup grated Parmesan cheese

Simmer until warm and well blended.
Serve over wide egg noodles.

Twice Baked Potato Casserole

5 medium to large russet potatoes, baked
10 pieces bacon, cooked crispy and crumbled
2 cups shredded cheddar cheese
1 cup grated Parmesan cheese
1 pt. sour cream
½ cup green onion, chopped
Salt
Pepper

Either dice whole cooked potatoes or scoop out inner potato and discard skin. Combine with remaining ingredients. Transfer to greased baking dish. Bake at 350 degrees for 50 minutes until bubbly and lightly browned.

Zoe's Quick and Easy Hash-Brown Casserole

Mix:

4 cups frozen shredded hash browns
4 cups broccoli florets
4 cups cooked and diced ham
2 cans nacho cheese soup
1 soup can of milk

Pour into 9 x 13 baking pan.

Top with 2 cups shredded cheddar cheese.

Bake at 425 degrees for 30–40 minutes.

Scalloped Ham and Potato Casserole

5–6 large potatoes, peeled and thinly sliced
2 cups cooked ham, cubed
1 cup grated cheddar cheese

Sauce:
Melt 1 stick butter (real butter, no substitutions) in saucepan over medium heat.

When melted add:
½ 8 oz. pkg. cream cheese
2 cups heavy whipping cream
Stir until cream cheese is completely dissolved.

Slowly add:
2 cups grated Parmesan cheese (the good stuff)
1 cup grated Romano cheese (add slowly; don't let it clump)
Stir until smooth.

Add:
1 tsp. ground nutmeg
½ tsp. garlic powder
Salt and pepper to taste.

Layer half potatoes, ham, and sauce in greased deep casserole dish. Repeat. Top with cheddar cheese.

Cook at 400 degrees for 45 minutes or until potatoes are tender.

Pulled Pork Verde

Place the following in a slow cooker set on high:
2–3 lbs. pork roast
2 cans (7 oz. each) diced green chilis
1 tbs. red pepper flakes
Water to cover

Cook until pork pulls apart easily (about 8 hours). Shred and use as filling for tacos or burritos.

Loco Moco

A traditional loco moco:

Sticky rice
Hamburger patty
Eggs, any style
Brown gravy

This easy sausage variation makes 8 servings:

Minute rice (4 cups rice/4 cups water)
8 precooked sausage patties
8 eggs, any style (I scramble)

Sausage gravy:
1 pkg. (16 oz.) ground sausage, browned
6 tbs. flour, shaken into 4 cups water

(I put water and flour into a plastic container with a lid and shake until flour is dissolved. Add to browned sausage. Simmer and stir until it thickens.)

Salt, pepper, and chili powder to taste

Place ⅛ rice on a plate. Layer on sausage patty over rice. Layer on 2 eggs. Cover with ⅛ sausage gravy.

I sometimes garnish with chopped green onions.

Chicken and Rice

Traditional chicken and rice
Combine:
1½ cups Minute rice
2 cans mushroom soup
2 soup cans milk
2 packets onion soup mix

Pour into greased 9 x 13 baking dish. Place 3–4 chicken breasts on top. Cover with foil.
Bake for 60 minutes at 350 degrees.
Remove foil and bake uncovered for an additional 20 minutes.

Cheesy chicken and rice
Combine:
1½ cups Minute rice
1 can cheddar cheese soup
1 jar Alfredo sauce
1 soup can milk

Pour into greased 9 x 13 baking dish. Place 3–4 chicken breasts on top. Cover with foil.
Bake for 60 minutes at 350 degrees.
Remove foil and bake uncovered for an additional 20 minutes.

Note: sometimes I spread shredded cheddar over the top after I remove the foil.

'Twas the night before Christmas and all through the house not a creature was stirring except my huge orange cat Marlow, who'd found the catnip Santa had left. In retrospect, I guess stuffing the cats' stockings before I went to bed wasn't the best idea I'd ever had. On the other hand, sitting in a silent  house with only the ticking of the grandfather clock and the crackling of the fire to trespass on the silence was kind of nice. Bella stayed upstairs with Zak, who was sleeping soundly, but Charlie followed me downstairs and was now curled up in my lap, twitching ever so gently as he acted out the parts in his little doggie dream.

Marlow and Spade are both lying on the rug in front of the fire playing with their new toys, although I can see Marlow eyeing the lights on the tree. He's been better this year about leaving the tree alone during the day, but at night, when the lights are twinkling brightly, he can hardly contain his impulse to take a closer look.

The full moon is reflecting off the lake as it shines brightly against the newly fallen snow. As I glance out the window to the beauty that surrounds me, I give a silent prayer of thanks for all I have and all that's to come in the upcoming year.

Desserts and Other Sweets

Ellie's Pumpkin Cheesecake

Rosie's Apple Crisp

Rosie's Pilgrim Pie

Zoe's Snowball Cookies

Ellie's Carrot Cake

Zoe's Pumpkin Snickerdoodles

Triple Chip Cookie Bars

Strawberry Angel Cake

Mini Cherry Cheesecake

Strawberry Jell-O Salad

Boysenberry Bars

Banana Cheese Pie

Fudge Sundae Pie

Easy Pineapple Upside-Down Cake

Choc-O-Lites

Mocha Ice Cream Pie

Ellie's Pumpkin Cheesecake

1 box graham cracker crust (follow directions on box to make 9 x 13 pan)
4 pkgs. cream cheese, softened
1½ cups sugar
16 oz. pumpkin
¾ cup whipping cream
3 tbs. flour
½ tsp. nutmeg
½ tsp. ginger
½ tsp. cinnamon
½ tsp. ground cloves
¼ tsp. salt
¼ tsp. vanilla
6 eggs

Beat together cream cheese and sugar. Add pumpkin, whipping cream, flour, spices, and vanilla. Mix. Add 4 whole eggs plus 2 egg yolks.

Pour over prepared graham cracker crust.
Bake at 325 degrees until toothpick comes out clean, about an hour. Refrigerate.

Topping:

½ cup sugar
2 cups whipping cream
½ cup powdered sugar
¼ tsp. vanilla

Whip until fluffy. Spread over chilled cheesecake.

Rosie's Apple Crisp

4 cups apples, peeled, cored, and sliced thin
1 cup cranberries
½ cup white sugar
2 tbs. cinnamon
2 tsp. ground nutmeg
½ cup quick cooking oats
½ cup flour
½ cup brown sugar
½ cup butter, cut into pieces
1 cup chopped pecans
1 jar caramel sauce (the kind used for ice cream is fine)

In a large bowl, mix apples, cranberries, white sugar, cinnamon, and nutmeg. Place in buttered 9 x 13 baking dish.

Combine oats, flour, and brown sugar. With a fork, mix butter in until crumbly.

Stir in pecans. Spread over apples. Drizzle with caramel sauce. Bake in preheated oven at 375 degrees for 40– 50 minutes or until apples are tender.

Serve with vanilla ice cream.

Rosie's Pilgrim Pie

1 premade pie shell

2 eggs
1 cup brown sugar
1 cup dark corn syrup
1 tsp. vanilla
2 tbs. butter, melted
⅛ tsp. salt
½ cup grated coconut
½ cup rolled oats
½ cup pecans

Beat eggs. Blend in sugar, corn syrup, vanilla, butter, and salt. Stir in coconut, oats, and pecans.

Pour into pie shell.

Bake at 400 degrees for 15 minutes. Reduce oven to 350 degrees and bake for 30 minutes.

Check with knife to see if pie is set. If not, set bake until set.

Zoe's Snowball Cookies

Mix thoroughly:
2 cups softened butter
1 cup powdered sugar
2 tsp. vanilla

Stir in:
4½ cups flour
1 tsp. salt

Add:
2 cups chopped walnuts

Refrigerate at least 1 hour.

Roll into 1-inch balls and place on ungreased baking sheet. Bake at 400 degrees until set but not brown. While still warm, roll in powdered sugar. Let cool and roll in powdered sugar a second time.

Ellie's Carrot Cake

3 eggs
2 cups sugar
3 cups finely shredded carrots
1 8 oz. pkg. softened cream cheese
1¼ cups vegetable oil
2 cups flour
2 tbs. ground cinnamon
2 tsp. baking soda
1 tsp. salt
1 can (8 oz.) crushed pineapple, well drained
2 cups walnuts, chopped

Beat eggs and sugar together until blended. Add carrots, cream cheese, and oil. Beat until smooth. Add dry ingredients. Stir in pineapple and nuts. Pour into greased 9 x 13 baking dish. Bake at 350 degrees for 55–60 minutes.

Frosting:

¾ cup butter, softened
6 oz. cream cheese, softened
1 tbs. vanilla
3 cups powdered sugar

Whip together and frost cake when cool; top with pecans.

Zoe's Pumpkin Snickerdoodles

1 cup butter at room temperature
1 cup granulated sugar
½ cup light brown sugar
¾ cup canned pumpkin
1 large egg
2 tsp. vanilla extract
3¾ cups flour
1½ tsp. baking powder
½ tsp. salt
½ tsp. ground cinnamon
¼ tsp. ground nutmeg

For the coating:

½ cup sugar
1 tsp. cinnamon
½ tsp. ground ginger
Dash of allspice

Whip together butter and sugars until creamy. Add pumpkin, egg, and vanilla. Mix well. Add dry ingredients and mix well.

Refrigerate for at least 1 hour.

In a separate bowl, mix the sugar and spices for the coating. Roll chilled dough into 1-inch balls. Roll in coating. Bake on ungreased cookie sheet at 400 degrees until lightly brown (around 12 minutes).

Triple Chip Cookie Bars

Graham cracker crust:
3 cups graham cracker crumbs
¾ cup melted margarine
½ cup sugar

Combine and press into 9 x 13 baking pan.

Middle Layer:
½ cup chocolate chips
½ cup butterscotch chips
1 can sweetened condensed milk (14 oz.)
1 tsp. vanilla

Microwave for 1 minute; stir, microwave 30 seconds more. Pour over crust.

Topping:
Remainder of large bag of chocolate chips (approx. 11 oz.)
Remainder of large bag of butterscotch chips (approx. 11 oz.)
1 cup white chocolate chips
1½ cups salted peanuts
Pour evenly over crust.

Bake at 350 degrees for 25 minutes.

Strawberry Angel Cake

Make angel food cake according to directions on box; bake in angel flute cake pan. Cool completely. Cut top off about 1 inch down. Scoop out middle, leaving adequate cake on sides.

Mix together:

1 small box strawberry Jell-O, made according to directions and chilled until set
⅓ small (8 oz.) Cool Whip
⅔ pt. (16 oz.) fresh strawberries, cut up small

Fill cake with Jell-O mixture; there will be some mixture left in most cases. Replace cake "lid" that was set aside. Frost with remaining Cool Whip. Garnish with remaining whole strawberries.

Mini Cherry Cheesecakes

Preheat oven to 350 degrees. Line cupcake pan with 12 liners.

Crust:

1½ cups graham cracker crumbs (or crushed cookie crumbs)
6 tbs. butter or margarine, melted
6 tbs. sugar

Mix together and fill bottom of 12 cupcakes.

Filling:

2 (8 oz.) pkg. of cream cheese, softened
¾ cup white granulated sugar
2 eggs
2 tbs. vanilla

Mix together until smooth and free of lumps. Divide between 12 cupcakes. Bake at 350 degrees for 15 minutes or until set.

Let mini cheesecakes cool completely, then top with cherry pie (or other fruit) filling.

Strawberry Jell-O Salad

2 small boxes strawberry Jell-O
16 oz. (about 2 cups) sliced strawberries
1 cup chopped walnuts

16 oz. sour cream

Mix:

1 small box Strawberry Jell-O (made per directions on box)
1 pint (16 oz.) sliced strawberries
1 cup chopped walnuts (add more if you really like nuts)

Pour into bottom of 9 x 13 glass baking dish. Chill until set (about 2 hours).

After first layer is set:

Spread 16-oz. container of sour cream over the top (don't use low fat). Chill for 30 minutes.

Make second small box of strawberry Jell-O according to directions. Carefully pour or ladle the Jell-O on top of sour cream layer; be careful when placing this layer on top or you'll mess up the sour cream. Chill for 2 hours.

Boysenberry Bars

Mix together:

2 cups flour
1½ cups long cooking oats
½ cup brown sugar, packed
1 cup butter (room temperature)

Reserve 1 cup of mixture. Press into greased 9 x 13 baking pan.

Cream together:

8 oz. cream cheese, softened
14 oz. can sweetened condensed milk
1 tsp. vanilla
1 pkg. (8 oz.) white chocolate chips

Spread over flour mixture.

Combine 1 can boysenberry pie filling (or any fruit). Mix with 2 tbs. cornstarch. Spread over cream cheese layer.

Sprinkle reserve flour mixture and 1 cup chopped salted cashews or peanuts over the top.

Bake at 375 degrees for 35–40 minutes or until golden.

Cool and cut into bars.

Banana Cheese Pie

2 large bananas

1 ready-made graham cracker crust (or make your own)

8 oz. cream cheese, softened

1 large box vanilla instant pudding

3 cups milk

1 small container Cool Whip

1 cup macadamia nuts, chopped

Slice bananas into piecrust. Mix cream cheese, pudding, and milk together and let set for 5 minutes. Pour over bananas in piecrust. Spread Cool Whip on top and garnish with macadamia nuts.

Fudge Sundae Pie

Crust:

¼ cup light corn syrup
2 tbs. brown sugar
3 tbs. butter
2½ cups Rice Krispies cereal

Combine corn syrup, brown sugar, and butter in saucepan. Cook over medium heat until it boils. Pour over Rice Krispies. Stir together and then press into buttered pie plate.

Topping:

½ cup peanut butter
½ cup chocolate fudge sauce
3 tbs. corn syrup
(Note: I often make extra topping and pile it on thick. It's up to you.)

Mix together and spread half on piecrust. Layer in softened ice cream. I use vanilla, but coffee or chocolate works as well. Spread other half of topping over top.

Freeze for 2–3 hours.

Easy Pineapple Upside-Down Cake

¼ cup butter or margarine
1 cup packed brown sugar
1 can (20 oz.) pineapple slices in juice, drained, juice reserved
1 jar (6 oz.) maraschino cherries without stems, drained
1 box yellow cake mix, eggs and oil called for on box

Heat oven to 350 degrees. In 9 x 13-inch pan, melt butter in oven. Sprinkle brown sugar evenly over butter. Arrange pineapple slices on brown sugar. Place cherry in center of each pineapple slice and arrange remaining cherries around slices; press gently into brown sugar.

Add enough water to reserved pineapple juice to match liquid called for on cake mix box. Make batter as directed on box, substituting pineapple juice mixture for the water. Pour batter over pineapple and cherries.

Bake 42–48 minutes (44–53 minutes for dark or nonstick pan) or until toothpick inserted in center comes out clean. Immediately run knife around side of pan to loosen cake. Place heatproof serving plate upside down onto pan; turn plate and pan over. Leave pan over cake 5 minutes so brown sugar topping can drizzle over cake; remove pan. Cool 30 minutes. Serve warm or cool. Store covered in refrigerator.

Choc-O-Lites

1 tbs. cocoa
2 cups sugar
½ cup butter
½ cup milk
½ cup peanut butter
1 tbs. vanilla
3 cups oatmeal

Bring cocoa, sugar, butter, and milk to full boil. Boil for 1 minute. Add the peanut butter and stir until melted. Remove from heat. Add vanilla and oatmeal. Stir well. Drop by teaspoonful onto waxed paper. Let cool.

Mocha Ice Cream Pie

Melt:
3 tbs. butter in saucepan

Add:
2 tbs. brown sugar
¼ cup corn syrup

Cook on medium heat until it boils. Pour over 2½ cups Rice Krispies cereal.
Press into buttered pie plate.

Mix together:
½ cup caramel sauce
½ cup peanut butter
3 tbs. corn syrup

Spread half on piecrust. Cover with softened coffee ice cream. Spread other half of sauce mixture on top.

Freeze for 2–3 hours.

Books by Kathi Daley

Come for the murder, stay for the romance.

Zoe Donovan Cozy Mystery:

Halloween Hijinks
The Trouble With Turkeys
Christmas Crazy
Cupid's Curse
Big Bunny Bump-off
Beach Blanket Barbie
Maui Madness
Derby Divas
Haunted Hamlet
Turkeys, Tuxes, and Tabbies
Christmas Cozy
Alaskan Alliance
Shamrock Shenanigans – March 2015

Paradise Lake Cozy Mystery:

Pumpkins in Paradise
Snowmen in Paradise
Bikinis in Paradise
Christmas in Paradise
Puppies in Paradise – February 2015

Whales and Tails Cozy Mystery:

Romeow and Juliet – January 2015

Road to Christmas Romance:

Road to Christmas Past

Kathi Daley lives with her husband, kids, grandkids, and Bernese mountain dogs in beautiful Lake Tahoe. When she isn't writing, she likes to read (preferably at the beach or by the fire), cook (preferably something with chocolate or cheese), and garden (planting and planning, not weeding). She also enjoys spending time on the water when she's not hiking, biking, or snowshoeing the miles of desolate trails surrounding her home. Kathi uses the mountain setting in which she lives, along with the animals (wild and domestic) that share her home, as inspiration for her cozy mysteries.

Stay up to date with her newsletter, *The Daley Weekly*. There's a link to sign up on both her Facebook page and her website, or you can access the sign-in sheet at: http://eepurl.com/NRPDf

Visit Kathi:
Facebook at Kathi Daley Books,
www.facebook.com/kathidaleybooks
Twitter at Kathi Daley@kathidaley
Webpage www.kathidaley.com
E-mail kathidaley@kathidaley.com

Made in the USA
San Bernardino, CA
28 January 2015